The Edelweiss a Poem

John R. Bolles

BIBLIOLIFE

THE

EDELWEISS:

A Poem

BY

JOHN R. BOLLES.

" Love, grace divine to mortals given,
Links heaven to earth and earth to heaven "

NEW LONDON:
CHARLES ALLYN.
1881.

The trembling bird will leave its nest
   When it has wings to fly,
So fluttering thoughts within my breast
   Seek immortality.

CONTENTS.

BOOK I.

Apostrophe to Connecticut. Reference to its history, scenery, customs, talent, wealth, &c. Early life of our hero and heroine. Charms of nature. Praise of love. Travels in foreign countries. Mabel's farewell to her native land. The correspondence of the lovers.

BOOK II.

Homeward bound. Mabel's song. A carrier Dove sets a ring on her finger. Message from Arthur. Mabel's reply. Arthur's thoughts, rhapsodies, &c. Mabel recalls past scenes. The shower. Shelter in a mill wheel. Sleigh ride. Wandering by a stream. Playful lambs. Among the trees. Bird's concert. Song of the robin. Mabel caught in a bramble. Arthur releases her. Further revelations. Meeting by the spring. Arthur's vivid impressions. A bird lights upon his hand. He gives it to Mabel. Raptures of love. Whirl in the mill wheel. Unexpected meeting. Jacob's Rock. Beneath the stars. Walk upon the street. He bids the sun stand still. Green hills. Meeting in a wild pasture.

BOOK III.

Satan's enticing proposition. Arthur's fidelity. Love's rhapsody. Beauty in the soul. Love a divine psalm. Embarking for home. Scene in foreign lands. Arthur's description. Mount Blanc. Volcanoes. The five lakes. Valleys and mountains of Switzerland. Antique villas. Simplon Pass. Above the clouds. Nature's wonders. Rome. The Pope's blessing. The Nile. Swimming the Hellespont. Galleries of art. Napoleon's grand army. Raphael's Madonna at Dresden. The Parthenon. Pyramids. Ireland. The Blarney stone. Scotland. Fair Ellen's isle. Arthur's praise of Mabel. Storm at sea. Mabel on tranquil waters. Her remembrance of the Bay of Naples. Sunrise and sunset. Venice. The Rhone. The Thames. Ships of war. Groton monument. New London. Ancient mill. John Rogers. Margarita First crossing of the Atlantic by steam. Vessels in the harbor. A night on Jacob's rocks Storm at sea. Arthur's vessel sinking. Mabel's vessel. Midnight. Rising moon. All lives saved. Meeting of the lovers. Bright skies. Mabel overboard. Rescue by Arthur. Safe arrival home. Consummation.

BOOK IV.

Matrimony ordained of God in the garden of Eden, and blessed by the presence of Christ. A visit to our hero and heroine after many years. Their love true and stainless. Green the earth and bright the skies. Their conversation concerning life, death, and immortality. Blendings of the earthly and the heavenly life. Nothing lost in nature or the human soul. Love beautiful in age. A flower of Paradise. Their faith and hope in God. Delight in Him. Earth the borderland of heaven. The city lighted by the glory of God.

INTRODUCTION.

Obedience to law is the glory of the Universe. When man shall conform to the moral and physical rule of his being, the wilderness will bud and blossom as the rose, harmony and happiness abound, Love reign in its true beauty, and God be honored in all His works. By examples of purity and goodness set before the mind, the heart is made better, while machinations, intrigues, and jealousies tend to an opposite result. The object of this work is to display in some degree at least, the grace and dignity of Love, which is not to be despised, but reverenced as the beneficent, beautiful creature of God, His gift in which He is to be glorified.

"Whatsoever things are pure, whatsoever things are lovely, whatsoever things are of good report, if there be any virtue, if there be any praise, think on these things."

J. R. B.

THE EDELWEISS.

BOOK I.

Fair land which borders on the Sound,
    That Broadway of the seas,
Where fleets of vessels trim their sails
    To court the favoring breeze,
Or steam away by night and day;—
    Long live thy memories!

Forever looking toward the South,
    And hailing summer sweet,
While half the commerce of the world
    Is passing at thy feet!—(1)
Fair land of learning, wealth, and power,
    Thy praises I repeat!

---

(1) See Appendix

1*

Thy rocks, thy hills, thy skies I sing,
　　And thy illustrious name,
From patriotic ancestry
　　Thy sons and daughters came ;
Thy Ledyards, Putnams, Lyons wreathe
　　The temple of thy fame !

Thy sturdy oaks, thy towering elms,
　　Majestic in their might,
The springs that from thy hill-sides gush,
　　All dancing with delight,
As on they flow through dales below,
　　And o'er the pebbles bright.

Thy rivers grand, thy valleys green,
　　Thine Indian Summer haze,
Thy clouds that fly on snow-white wings,
　　Thy golden Autumn days,
Thy buds of Spring, thy birds of song,
　　Resplendent sunset rays !

Thine ancient loom and spinning-wheel,
　　Thy hunts for fox and coon,
Thy waving fields, thy bending sheaves,

Thy glorious harvest moon ;
Thy meadows dappled o'er with flowers,
   Thy morning, evening, noon !

Thy winter fires e'er burning bright,
   Reflected on the wall,
And faces lit with heavenly light
   To cheer and welcome all,—
Like dew which fell on Hermon's mount,
   Blessings upon thee fall !

Let thy fair fame in glory rise
   With every new-born day.
Thy banner waving to the skies,
   Its stars and stripes display
Before the world's admiring eyes
   Till skies shall pass away.

Mabel went tripping forth one morn
   So blithesome o'er the dews,
To catch their glow and watch the buds
   Unfolding vestal hues,
There Arthur met her on the lawn,
   Elate with welcome news.

"The Captain's ship comes through the Race,
    With all her sails outspread,
Her signal streaming from the mast,
    The Burgee white and red!"

Now all the house is filled with joy
    And rapture running o'er,
And pattering feet are first to greet
    The father at the door!

And childhood's merry voices rang
    To cheer the happy morn,
As once the stars together sang
    When a new world was born!

Through woodland pastures where she roamed
    To listen to the birds,
On Mabel's ear there sometimes stole
    Sweetest of human words.

And as her fingers softly swept
    The soul-entrancing lyre,
The echoes of an absent voice
    Would happiest notes inspire.

In fancy's bright, ethereal web
　All dipped in rainbow dyes,
Were blent the beauty of the Earth
　And glory of the skies.

The broad, smooth green that stretched before
　The village church, the school,
Where well they conned their lessons o'er,
　Or felt the master's rule,

The crimson dawn of early morn,
　And tints of closing day,
The flocks that rambled o'er the hills,
　The skipping lambs at play,

And all the social gatherings,
　Huskings and rustic " Bees,"
The trout they took from sylvan brook,
　And nuts from forest trees,

Still more the fond cordialities
　That loving hearts inspire,
A father's voice, a mother's smile,
　The hearthstone and the fire,

Are pictured in their memories,
　Where they will ever be,
Part of the soul's immortal life
　As drops are of the sea.

Though wending on their lonely way
　Or in the crowded mart,
They ne'er forget the love that set
　Its signet on their heart.

O Love! the whitest rose of heaven,
The fairest charm to earth that's given;
Light of the soul, celestial flame!
Touched by live coal I'd speak thy name;
Dwell ever in my heart as young
As when creation's song was sung,
And God with man at evening talked,
And midst the trees of Eden walked.
Thy starry chain is ever bright,
Its links are bars of rosy light,
The cunning work of angel hands,
Nor time nor space can loose its bands.

With love, angelic love, their guide,
    Beneath the bending skies,
If words were meant their thoughts to hide,
    They could not hide their eyes:
While waving trees and wooing breeze
    Trilled notes of Paradise.

Days, months, and years roll on apace,
And sunny fortune lends its grace,
Fair art with all its charm delights,
And learning to its seat invites,
While friendly counsels bid them go
To distant lands and wiser grow.

MABEL'S GOOD-BYE

" Good-bye to the land of the free,
    The home of the true and the brave!
    O, welcome the sparkling blue sea,
    And welcome the plume-tossing wave!
    Good-bye to the rocks and the brooks,
    The orchard, the well-sweep, and grove;
    Good-bye to the valleys and nooks,
    But not to the hearts that I love. "

Still on the liquid numbers flow,
" To summer's shade and autumn's glow,
To bending trees enrobed in snow,
All glistening in the moonlight's tinge,
As nature weaves her crystal fringe,
Or airy sylphs, with beaming eyes,
Besprinkling diamonds from the skies,
Have set upon each bud and stem
Its more than royal diadem ·—
But thou, O Sun, wilt shine as bright,
And thou, O moon, shed gentle light;
Aurora Borealis too,
Shall shoot swift arrows 'thwart the blue,
Feathered with rays of varied hue —
To these I need not bid adieu.
And all the pure, harmonious throng
    That I am wont to see,
Sublimely bursting into song,
    Shall waft their strains to me ;
And with that host I am content
Wherever I may be;
And still my heart shall beat in tune
With their high symphony."

As birds abroad on lightsome wing
One song will still be singing,
As on the hill and in the vale
Alike the flowers are springing
And on the breath of morn and eve
Sweet perfumes ever flinging—
Though wide apart yet one in heart
Their thoughts with·love are ringing.

Fair as the rays of morning bright
Pure as the source of rosy light,
And fadeless as the stars above
Blooms in the soul immortal love.
'Tis watered by perennial spring
'Tis sheltered 'neath the Almighty's wing
And over it the angels sing.

But many loves appear around
Like transient buds upon the ground,
Which never were for fruit designed
And blooming quick are out of mind,
These may have place within the heart
And to the soul a grace impart.

Call thou not by that holy name
A lurid, false, and fickle flame,
A meteor flashing on the night
To vanish ever out of sight.
From love which boldly makes display
Before the world, we turn away,
Devoid of decency and sense
It is not love ; it's impudence.—
The hidden juices of the vine
Impart the flavor to the wine,
And choicest scents of roses rare
Are borne upon the twilight air.

By the most sacred ties entwined,
Long had our lovers' hearts enshrined
A secret, which they dared not tell,
Lest it should break the witching spell.

As richest veins of ore concealed,
Wait their abundant store to yield.

" My daughter," once an artist said,
" To the best painter shall be wed."—

Inspired, a blacksmith gained the art
And took the fair one to his heart.

Love taught the smith to paint so well,
　For wonders love can do ;
Though artists picture him as blind,
　All arts he can pursue.

He with his talismanic wand
　Can make one heart of two,
And e'er you are aware, perchance
　His spell is over you !

And now to capture Mabel's heart
With Arthur's pen, love plies his art.

ARTHUR TO MABEL

Two clouds appeared one summer's day
Lightly drifting on their way
All roseate blushing in the sun,—
I looked again and they were one.

Two drops of opalescent dew
Glances at each other threw,
My heart with secret wonder cried,
The dew drops are in love allied.

Two stars shone forth in yonder skies,
Looking in each other's eyes,
And whispering in each other's ears,
Love binds in chains the heavenly spheres!

Two robins came in early spring,
Dulcet notes I heard them sing,
Together built their hidden nest,
Love's ruby seal upon their breast.

I saw two doves light by a door,
Cooing their fond lesson o'er ;
Where is the dove that flies to me,
That so delights my heart to see ?

Could I but sail in phantom boat,
Or on the wing of zephyr float,
I'd find, down in the meadow sweet,
The flowers that sprang thy steps to greet,
    Hid from the vulgar eye,
The spot that lightsome foot had pressed,
Of all the world the loveliest,
    Where the young beauties lie !

A wild rose blossomed on its bush ;
I saw it when it caught thy blush ;
A glory on the thicket set,
Within my soul 'tis blooming yet.

MABEL TO ARTHUR.

I know the voice that calls to me,
A lonely wanderer o'er the sea,
So sweetly sounding in my ear,
Its distant echoes still I hear.

The clouds that float upon the air,
The dewdrops sparkling everywhere,
The robin redbreast and the dove
Are emblems eloquent of love.

For love the constellations sing
And Cygnus spreads his mighty wing.
The Pleiades and Orpheus' lyre
Forever glow with purest fire,
And all the flowers in beauty set
Are letters in love's alphabet.

Shall I again behold his face,
Again those hills and valleys trace ?

Pluck four-leaved clover from its bed ;—
Shall I with him the forest tread,
Where, in life's early hour we strayed,
And with the rippling waters played,
And harkened at the hollow trees
To hear the humming of the bees,
Hailing the red rose on its bush,
Catching the evening's peaceful hush?
I'd seek those woods, I'd find the birds
That sang for him melodious words,
That bough on which he carved my name,
Where scarce another footstep came,
Close hidden for his eye alone,—
(I saw it when the leaves had flown).
There ever murmuring runs the rill,
There Nature's anthem rises still!

Like golden apples falling round,
These pleasant words give gladsome sound,
As struck from silver chiming bells,
Or springing up from music's wells,
His glowing breast its rapture tells!

ARTHUR TO MABEL.

Fly, fly to my bosom, thou beautiful one!
The joy of my being, my morning, my noon;
The fairest of colors that flash from the sun,
My jasmine, my myrtle, my blossom of June,
My evening, my twilight, my moonlight, my star,
My dewdrop, my snowdrop, my rainbow you are,
My rose and my lily, my violet blue,
My timid arbutus of delicate hue,
My spring, summer, autumn, with glory bedight,
My jewel of winter, my Edelweiss white,
My bird of bright plumage, of beautiful wing,
My field and my forest, where all the birds sing,
My blush of Aurora, my bloom of the tree,
My wealth of Golconda, my wave of the sea,
My splendor of sunset, zodiacal light,
That sits as a queen at the threshold of night,
All beauties of nature are centered in thee.
The pearls from the ocean, the gems from the dell,
All beauty in nature my love doth excel!

There's charm in the voice that comes over the hills
No nightingale's carol such sweetness distils,

Mellifluous accents are borne on the breeze,
As sounds from a harp hanging high in the trees;
Divine inspiration breathes forth in each word,
In each little letter the song of a bird,
That rarest of voices that ever was heard:—
Oh, had I the wings, the fleet wings of a dove,
I'd scale the high mountains, I'd fly to my love.

MABEL TO ARTHUR.

There's splendor in the morning hour,
    There's glory in the sun,
Twin roses blossom in the bower,
    Dew-drops together run,
Two rivers meet and laughing greet,
    And murmur, "we are one."

The day is breaking brightly round,
    Away the shadows flee,
The flowers appear upon the earth,
    The blossoms on the tree,
And chirping birds sing out their words,
    In chorus merrily.

And Ocean's shells and sounding bells,
And Spheres which chime their tones sublime
  In purest harmony,—
Lute that Apollo's fingers stirred—
But to my ear the sweetest word
  Is his who speaks to me.

Stoop down, ye heavens, to bless my love!
  To speed him on his way!
And ye bright orbs in concert move,
  Nor in your circuit stay;
And thou, O chariot of the sun!
  Bring round the welcome day.

Love's crystal cup is brimming o'er,
And still their thoughts together pour
Like wavelets meeting on the shore.
Part of that great unfathomed deep
That doth perpetual silence keep:—
Like strains of music wafted near,
From Arthur Mabel waits to hear.
She asks "What can the reason be?
I know he's not forgotten me:

  2

My letter's lost, he waits," she cries.
Then from her hand this missive flies.

"And did your pen forget to write?
 I'm watching for the morning light."
 This answer came, a brighter flame
 Ne'er rose upon a darker night!
' Your letters both I have received,
 That mine was lost do not be grieved,
 The hand that penned it is the same,
     The heart that did indite it
 Is burning with as constant flame,—
     The will that bade me write it
 Is true and strong as yonder sun,
 That never failed his course to run,
 And never yet was found too late
 To lift the latch of morning's gate:—
 Were I but where my thoughts abide
 I should be nearest to thy side!"
Thus Arthur hastily replied.

And now to Mabel's hand is brought
The letter she had vainly sought.

THE LOST LETTER

I've often wondered why the moon
Shone out with so much splendor;
They say it borrows from the sun,
Of light the glorious lender.
But I am certain that I might
A better reason render;
The fairest charm the moon e'er wore
I saw my darling send her!
The new moon stole sweet smiles one night,
  Yet I made no complaint,
I thought her pilfering was right,
  And would be in a saint,—
The new moon stole! O little jade!
Her loveliest grace from earth's fair maid,
  Delighted to behold her;
And this may be the reason why
(For love's conceits rise very high)
So oft I seek the western sky,
  Just over my right shoulder.

The constellations clearer shine,
With closer tendrils clings the vine,

The insect's tinsel wings unfold,
A richer purple, green, and gold,
Since all thy heart to me is told.
The gorgeous sunsets are more bright,
More opal-tinted morning's light,
Sweeter the breath of new-mown hay,
With nimbler feet the young fawns play,
The moss rose has a deeper blush,
The evening hour a gentler hush,
With fresher hues the vales are decked,
The lake doth more of heaven reflect.

Where lofty mountains touch the skies
I plucked for thee this Edelweiss [2.]
That blooms amid eternal snows,
And fear of winter never knows.

Listen to Mabel's charmed reply :—
" Darkness hás vanished from my sky ;
Pillows on which angels dream,
Fleecy clouds more fleecy seem,
A lighter shadow casts the trees,
And choicest pearls enrich the seas,

The day-star shines with clearer rays,
Birds twitter earlier songs of praise,
A tribute to creation's King,
Sweet-briers more of sweetness fling.
There's glory in the azure skies,
But more of glory in those eyes
Whose mystic depths I long to see,
They found that Edelweiss for me!

BOOK II.

As homeward now their faces turn,
From Lyons Mabel, he from Berne,
The post no more can bring their words,
But in their hearts are singing birds,
Sweet little birds which find no rest,—
Trembling, fluttering in their nest,
Or pouring out their winsome strain;—
Mabel takes up the glad refrain.

"I'll sing to my love as he sails o'er the sea,
I know at this moment he's thinking of me;
I'll sing to the ocean to bear him along,
I'll sing to the breezes to waft him my song,
I'll sing to the billows to give him no rest,
Till like a wild hart he shall bound to my breast,
I'll sing to the skies that beheld him embark ;
My song shall ascend with the song of the lark,
That warbles its hymn at the earliest dawn,
As zephyrs are stirred at the touch of the morn."

(31)

And what did she do, with the fancies that flew
Away like the sunbeams in heaven's broad blue ?
They are penciled on paper of violet shade
And pressed to her bosom as rose leaves they're
  laid.

Sitting in a rural bower,
Pensive at the twilight hour,
At her feet has just alighted,
Carrier pigeon all delighted
With the tidings it has brought,
Token of the love that's plighted :—
Quicker than the wings of thought,
In her hand the bird was caught ;
From its neck she took a ring,
Listen !   Hear the diamond sing !
" Brighter than the stars above
 On the waves of light I glide,
 Nature's purest seal of love,
 With you always to abide.
 I am from your lover sent ! "—
Mabel's heart is now content.

To greet his eyes a glad surprise
To Arthur's hand this answer flies.
"Let the sweetest doves attend thee!
Angels from above defend thee!
God, His blessing ever send thee!
Safely borne across the sea.
On that shore keep watch for me,
A golden band upon my hand
I there will give you greeting.
O, bird fly quickly o'er the land
The moments are so fleeting.
Within his soul, he'll understand
His name I am repeating
And that his brow with bliss be fanned
I always am entreating.
    Benignant powers
    Which rule the hours
Haste on the joyful meeting."

ARTHUR'S SOLILOQUY.

Walking lonely on the street,
One there was I chanced to meet,
Dust beneath her steps was gold,
All my heart did her infold.

It was in the month of June,
Morning rose on highest noon,
Heaven and earth together met,
Blending glories exquisite,—
Tangled in love's mazy spell,
Which was heaven I could not tell.

Of late a gentle shower of rain
    Had fallen on the earth,
Now all was fair and bright again,
    As nature at her birth.

We met, we passed, but not to me
    Were turned those radiant eyes,
For they were looking steadfastly
    Upon the clear blue skies.

Beneath her free, elastic tread
    Earth wore a lighter grace;
The heavens were brighter overhead
    That saw her smiling face.

Love's blissful rays were in my soul concentered,
Through beauty's lens they found their way and
        entered;

A golden silence filled the earth and sky,
Glad nature worshiped her, and why not I?

All clad was my love in the purest of white;
The moon in her splendor, the stars, ever bright,
Ne'er dawned on the world with such ravishing
      light.
Shine on, O thou fair one, with up-glancing eyes!
The seal in thy soul of its own native skies;—
Thou hast opened the windows of heaven to me,
Descending to us, the white angels I see!
In her clear vestal pride they fly by her side,
And catch a sweet glimpse of those eyes as they
      glide;—
Her bosom the palace of loftiest thought,
Her spirit, the chalice with glory inwrought,
To which all the fairest of lilies are brought,
Of lilies the rarest the angels e'er sought.
Shine on, O thou proud one! so silent and true,
Perceiving, reflecting each beautiful view.
Not a bud on the tree, not a cloud in the skies,
Can escape the swift glance of those heart-piercing
      eyes.

Thy presence makes brighter a glad world like this,
My heart is made lighter, my cup filled with bliss.
I'd stamp on a miter thy feet but to kiss!
Those eyes from the skies are now turning to me.
In them all of glory celestial I see.
On her garment's neat hem the tiniest gem,
I'd wear it forever in Love's diadem;
'Twas but dust on the stone a moment before,
'Tis a part of the sun on the one I adore!

The depths of the stream I would ford for my love.
I'd pluck the bright stars in my hand, as from Jove!
I'd climb the tall mount to its snowy white peak,
To hear but one word that my darling might speak;
As lightly I'd bound as the sprightly red deer,
If to her the least whisper of danger were near.
Let loud thunders rattle, let swift lightnings fall,
Let hailstones give battle, I'd sport with them all;
The stars in their courses, I'd count them as naught.
The stars in their courses, that Sisera fought!
The sun shall awake from his sleep in the morn,
His horses, his chariot, I hold them in scorn,
For, deep in my heart does a fairer light dawn,

But all the bright forces in nature are mine,
The stars, in their courses, all bow at Love's shrine.

In noontide glow I met her so,
    The blue skies bending o'er her,
And rarest loves and whitest doves
    Paused in their flight before her;
Then all my heart took rapturous part
    With nature to adore her!

We see the beauty of the flower,
    But not its fragrance sweet.
More bliss was garnered in that hour
    Than language can repeat.

    That vision so bright
    Still dwells on my sight,
        'Tis present before me ever,
    As when she passed by
    With her heaven-lit eye.
        Can I forget it? No, never!

MABEL'S SOLILOQUY.

By ancient mill, tall trees around, (3)
Where waters fall with dashing sound
Over the rocks in rapid flow,
Foaming and leaping as they go,
Sequestered, yet within the city,
A passing cloud on us took pity,
Or rose on purpose for our sake.
Foreboding thunder bade us take
A shelter in the great mill-wheel,
Love does for us such chances steal!
'Twas very still, and so were we,
As Dryads nestled in a tree,
When suddenly we heard a sound!
The wheel began to turn around!
Where I was whirled, how can I tell?
I knew within whose arms I fell.
He caught me! Like a wild gazelle
On Syrian hill, with fleetest bound
He set my feet upon the ground.

Riding out in tricksy sleigh,
  Four of us one night,

Over hills and through the dells;
Merrily, merrily rang the bells
　And the moon was bright.
How it was I cannot say,
On a bank of snow we lay,
　In a jolly plight.
Silver bells rang out anew,
O'er the hills again we flew.

By a streamlet once we strolled,
Cowslips blossomed bright as gold,
Dandelions, violets blue,
Fresh within that dingle grew,
But in my heart was sweeter thought,
Than all the beauteous flowers had brought.
He took me up, I scarcely knew it,
There was but one that saw him do it—
He took me up as partridge feather
And we crossed o'er the stream together.

White are the footsteps of the light,
　But whiter was the blossom,
He brought to me among the hills,—
　I wore it in my bosom.

Close by a little babbling spring
Where daisies throng and wild birds sing,
The swallow and the bobolink
Oft come to dip their wing or drink,.
And humming-birds were flitting round,
I seemed to hear another sound ;
It was a footstep, chanced to be
Of one who spied me 'neath a tree,
Which spread abroad its leafy wings ;
'Tis there the oriole's nest we see ;—
And harp Eolian lightly sings ;—
With robin Red-breast in his hand.
" How did you catch it ? "   " Understand,
It flew to me," my heart would say,
" My love has flown to me to-day."

'Twas the robin did begin it,
Merry birds sang carol round,
Thrush and blackbird in a minute,—
Trees were vocal with the sound.
All the warblers took a part:
Bluebird, mocking-bird, and linnet,
Each one sang unto my heart,
But the robin sings within it.

I know full well the day and hour,
  He in the pasture found me,
Entangled in a thorny bower,
  And how his hand unbound me,
Then as he swiftly fled away,—
My heart was hoping he would stay.

ARTHUR'S SOLILOQUY.—(Continued.)

Stately, queenly, modest, sweet,
Did I then an angel meet?
Looking always to the sky,
Rapt in thoughts and fancies high,
Picture in my soul displayed,
There to live, and ne'er to fade,
More than all my heart could hold,
Wings of Dove, inlaid with gold!
Does she mean to hide away?
Will she not those charms display?
Glancing round with sprightly grace,
A Goddess! I behold her face.
Flashed upon me those bright eyes,
I looked into Paradise!

Portals of celestial day!
Founts of blissful ecstacy!
Glimpses of her soul I see,
In those eyes that pour on me
Sparks of fire or sparks of being,
I admire, I turn from seeing.
All the pure refulgencies,
All the sweetest radiances
Met and mingled in those glances.
Diamonds shine not half so bright,
Clearest stars have no such light.
'Twas as if all sparkling dews,
Rays from all prismatic hues,
All of nature's fairest dyes,
All the world's resplendencies,
Clustering dazzled in those eyes;
All that could from ocean rise,
Or be borrowed from the skies;—
The dust was taken from the sun,
When thou wert formed, O matchless one!
Glories too ineffable,
Then upon my vision fell!
Beaming, streaming ever, ever!
Was there e'er such beauty?   Never!

Brilliancies ! and all for me,
Which no other one could see.
Those eyelashes, through which flashes
Every pure and peerless ray,
Eyelids fair as dewy morn,
Smiling East where day is born!
Turn from me those eyes away !
O, Nature, was thy art not spent,
When to my heart such charms were lent?
Then of heaven I had a view,
All the world was clad anew,
Waves of beauty, waves of gold,
Wings of light in me unfold,
More lustrous than the Butterfly's,
That deftly sought the flower,
That caught a glimpse of Beauty's eyes,
Within her leafy bower,
Or like the bird of Paradise
That always seeks the sky,
And never on the earth alights,—
With love's bright wings I fly.

I saw a little ringlet
    Tossing beside her face,

As if to hide a dimple,
　Love's secret dwelling-place ;—
There were a thousand dimples there,
I envied them that lock of hair ;
　　　Upon her neck
　　　Which graces deck
Love laid his witching snare.
Did she look down that I might spy
Those curls that nestled there ?

As passing near her home one night,
　Upon the window lay
A very soft and mellow light,
　Fair as the dawn of day,
Aladdin's lamp it might have been,
　I care not for the name,
Within my heart the thoughts of one,
　Awoke a fairer flame.

When fondest zephyr greets my face,
　The memory it brings,
Of one who moved her fan with grace,
　As butterfly its wings.

That smile where heaven had left its trace,
   My heart forever sings.

The crescent moon upon the sky,
   The verdure 'neath my feet,
All whisper to me " Love is high,"
   All whisper " Love is sweet."
And all the voices of the day,
   And voices of the night;—
The shells that murmur of the sea,
   Whatever charms the sight,
The morn awak'ning in the east,
   The evening's tender light,
To me their wondrous speech impart,
       Soul refining,
       Ever twining
Mightiest cords around my heart !
Blooming as by fairy spell,
Every flower the brightest pink,
In that deep, secluded dell
Where she came, a Nymph, to drink;
Every blossom doubly sweet,—
Bubbling spring by fountain fed,
Gurgling over rocky bed,

Leaping up the lips to greet,
There it was we chanced to meet,
Where we never met before ;
Rippling waters running o'er,
Rippling over dainty feet.
But she never raised her eye,
Did she know that I was nigh?

Fashioned for me in the morn of creation,
 Bathed in the fairest of dew,
  My darling so sweet
  With her lily-white feet
Dipped in the fountain anew ;
Quicker than the winds that blew,
Then I turned away mine eyes,
Looking upward to the skies.

There I stood on happy ground,—
Wistful zephyrs held me bound
For I might not rudely press
Onward to such loveliness,
So by flowing drapery hidden,
Scarce by modesty forbidden,
How I tried to steal away,
But my steps would not obey :

Just as if my thoughts it knew,
Or to tell me what to do,
Darting from the feathered band
A robin lighted on my hand.
I would call the bird by name,
For it fans to clearer flame
In my heart a joy so pure,
That it ever must endure.

Then I sped with gladdened pace
Where the blossoms bent with grace,
Violets and eglantine,
Forest glories all divine,
Velvet pansies tinged with gold
Tender thoughts to me unfold,
Silken cords around me twine:
Radiant joys about me spring,
I am touched with beauty's wing.
One there was I gave it to,
" Here's a bird belongs to you,
Take it, robin with red breast,"—
Coyest lips to mine were pressed !
   All thrilled were the trees,

And I heard my heart say,
" I've found where the bees
      Gather honey to-day!"
Every leaf the prettiest grew,
Every bud had fresher hue,
Lightly then the robin sped
To the branches overhead ;
Through the boughs its clear notes rang,
All the birds in concert sang,
All the winds in chorus blew,
And the trees were joyful too,
Happier words to me were sung,
Flowing from cherubic tongue ·—
Attentive worlds stoop down to hear!
Aloft to bear from sphere to sphere
The tones that so entranced mine ear,
For heaven itself would lose a note,
If those sweet strains should cease to float
Forever on the boundless sea,
Of glory through eternity.

Who says that anything can die
Worthy of heaven?   It is not I.

What royal colors hath the bow
And will they ever cease to glow ?
Behold the circling orbs of light,
And comets coming back to sight,—
As in the changing alphabet
All language eloquent is set,
Or in the grand kaleidoscope
   Where each delightful view,
Though varying a thousand times
   Again appears anew ;—
Bright'ning all its secret cells,
In the soul all beauty dwells.

Pebbles glancing in the stream,
Now as brilliant diamonds gleam—
Diamonds of the purest water,
(They had looked at Beauty's daughter !)
Softest mosses 'neath my tread,
Harps Eolian o'er my head.
Flashing eyes flashed clearest rays,
Blazing set my heart ablaze,
Every twinkling beam the brightest
Shot from jeweled quiver lightest !
   3

Darkening clouds involve the skies,
Thunders crash and lightning flies.
From the tempest's sudden shock
We are sheltered 'neath a rock.

Months and days had passed by, then
On a time we met again
Near a pond by Winthrop's mill,
While the wheel was standing still,
There to shun a shower we steal.
   Love has my thanks
   For all his pranks,
And for the turning of the wheel!
Rushing torrent o'er us pours,
Loud and louder yet it roars,
As were opened all the doors—
Doors and windows of the sky.
Never floods arose so high!
We were set in rapid motion.
Tidal wave or swell of ocean?
What's the matter?   Who can tell?
In my outstretched arms she fell!
That instant I remember well—

With quickest step I held my place.
Lifted aloft, she dropped with grace;
Dripping, she sank into my arms.
'Twas then I held a world of charms!
Many waters sounding o'er us,
Love poured out his mighty chorus.
Still the great mill-wheel would go—
'Tis going now for aught I know;
But in less than half a minute
Neither one of us were in it.

Coming quickly down the street,
Round the corner, one I meet.
Suddenly my heart-was stirred,
Fluttering, I caught a bird;
Cupid, from his bow, well bent,
All his arrows on me spent,
With a wily, gleeful eye,
Crying, as with laughter rent,
" Didst not know that I was by !"
When upon the street we walked,
('Twas not often) as we talked,
Then I bade the viewing sun
Cease his glorious course to run,

As on Gibeon's lofty hill
He for Joshua stood still!

Sweeter than canary birds,
Chattering their sweetest words.
Lisping music, soft and clear,
Fell a voice upon mine ear.
In its ruby picture set,
Each syllable a violet,
Or like a bud revealing more
Of loveliness it had in store,
Than all the world had seen before:
So did that mouth of wondrous mould
Its witching melody unfold—
Chained fast I stood at glory's door!
And still my heart its nectar sips
From coral, dainty parted lips!
And still the dulcet echoes roll
Throughout the chambers of my soul;
Those strains I never can forget,
But O! her thoughts were sweeter yet,
Locked within the heart's deep shrine,
Ever whispering, I am thine.

Move on, O Sun! Stand still no more!
Transport us to that happy shore,
Where first we heard the whipporwill
Singing beside the wood-girt hill,
And listened to the insect's trill.

On a clear day, the zephyrs play,
  As off we sail together,
A party small, of seven in all,
  Regardless of the weather;
The winds arose, the tempest blows,
  An isle of rocks is near us, (4)
Upcast on it, we climbing sit,
  With all the stars to cheer us.
Our little bark was swept away;—
We tarried till the break of day,
  Beneath those skies resplendent,
A brighter light through all that night
  Was in my soul ascendant.

Once among the hills I found her,
Whitest lambs were gamboling round her,
Then with all my heart I crowned her;

  5*

In my hand I held a blossom,
Eden's star upon her bosom!

I met my darling on a day
 Far out in a wild pasture,
Or overtook her, I might say,
 By going rather faster—
There sing the cuckoo and bluejay,
 And blooms the purple aster;—
In pressing through a narrow way,
 A bramble close had caught her;
Then swiftly as the lightning's play
 My hand assistance brought her.
Roses white and roses red

All around their perfume shed,
Violets peeping from their bed,
 As angel eyes had sought her!
Beauty there her robe had spread—
As then in haste away I fled,
As like an antelope I sped,
How comely are thy feet, I said,
 With shoes, O prince's daughter!

BOOK III.

SATAN TO ARTHUR.

Kings' daughters shall before you stand,
A queenly, fair, and glittering band,
And you shall have the power to choose;
Will you each one of them refuse?
With promise that your hand shall hold
At its command a mount of gold,
And you shall ride the royal beast
And with Ahasuerus feast,
Will you not hesitate at least?

ARTHUR

Set all these gifts before mine eye,
    And on my head a crown,
Or tell me I must surely die
On Haman's gallows lifted high
    Beneath a kingly frown,
My darling closer would I hold
And nearer to my heart enfold.

(55)

ARTHUR (*alone*).

Great waters cannot quench true love
   Nor sweeping simoons smoother;
Mine eyes I will not turn away
   To look upon another.
Though in the rock's deep cleft thou art,
   Or hid in secret place,
Thy voice to me is always sweet,
   Thy countenance is grace.

In a glad stream all nature flows,
Down in the dell there blooms a rose,
Which puts a greater glory on
Than e're was worn by Solomon.
Though kings may boast of royal line
A nobler royalty is mine;
Nor can their paltry treasures buy
The pearl, that in my soul doth lie.

I kiss each letter of her name,
As brilliant of the purest flame;
I love to murmur each sweet word,
That ever from her lips I've heard,
Repeating it, as mocking bird;

Lips dropping honey, music's spell,
Which he who loves, must love so well.

O rarest of loves!
O fairest of doves!
I'd pluck up a mountain
And toss it to Mars;
I'd drink up a fountain,
I'd stand on the stars,
I'd leap o'er the billowy sea:
Thou art clothed with the sun
O, my radiant one,
All beautiful art thou to me!

Love is a psalm which God hath made,
Chanted where'er his law's obeyed.
Who hearkens always to his voice,
And makes his will his only choice,
Hath right to immortality,
And every fruit of life's fair tree.
All thine are mine, and mine are thine,
The soul repeats in strains divine:
All things are holy to our touch
For God to us hath made them such.

Descend, O Love! on thy glad wing,
  The solitary place shall ring;
The wilderness shall incense fling,
  The watchman on thy walls shall sing.

As man from sin's deep curse is saved,
Earth is for him with glory paved;
He stands, an angel in the sun,
Whose will, with God's sweet will is one.
Large is the debt that sin has made,
Redemption all that debt has paid,
But purity of life we see,
Where'er its healing waters be.
Why the whole heart does he require?
That thou mayest touch the golden lyre;
And as a field the Lord doth bless
Blossom in all righteousness.
Keeping God's holy law in sight,
Thy body shall be full of light:
He took the same who for us died
And now, in heaven, is glorified.

Obedient to celestial force,
Law rules the planets in their course,
As with high messages they run,
Held in their circuits to the sun.
Despising law we lose our way,
Like wandering stars, forever stray.
How art thou fallen in darkness of night
Son of the morning, Lucifer bright!

It is a part of God's high plan,
That thou shouldst show thyself a man;
Without true manhood thou wilt be
A mollusk through eternity.
The viper's sting shall pierce the breast
In which the viper is caressed.
St. Paul of pure immortal fame
Shook the foul reptile to the flame;
Bid sin's more horrid brood retire
To their own lake of burning fire.
Denying self, bearing the cross,
Of earthly good, sustaining loss;
Sorrow and suffering and pain
Bring hallowed blessings in their train,
And evil in the heart is slain.

The crystal gate thine eyes shall see,
Where angels wait to welcome thee.
Seek good, 'twill come on swiftest wing,
The rock's inhabitant shall sing,
Love's alabaster box shall break,
Thine head the holy ointment take,
Thy face as angel's face shall shine,
And thou shalt drink of heavenly wine.

O God, inspire my soul to see
That all of beauty dwells in thee,
And thou hast set its bud in me,
The bud of holiness and truth
To blossom in unfading youth.

How great is his goodness,
How great is his beauty!
The pathway of love
Is the pathway of duty.
God gave to us eyes,
He will give us the rose,
The cup of salvation
For us overflows.
There's beauty of thought,

There's beauty of speech,
And beauty of soul,
Which thought cannot reach;
As a luminous stone
More of light will supply,
Than ever was brought
To the sight of the eye.
With richest of honors
Be love ever crowned.
All fruits of Pomona
In blossoms are found,
The bloom of our being
Deep tinted with heaven,
As fair day departing
With blushes of even!

Love's universe is very wide,
The world's are waiting by his side;
In the sun's chariot he will ride,
Or step upon the milky way
Up to the golden gates of day.
He with Arcturus' Sons will talk,
While on the earth we see him walk;

He gives the heavens a clearer glow,
Adds brighter luster to the bow,
And whiteness to the driven snow,
And glory to the human soul.
It is by love thou art made whole—
Let his immortal song be sung,
As honey dropping from the comb,
For glorious love is always young,
And sparkling as the white sea foam.

He takes the sunset's royal hues,
And mingling them with morning dews
Drinks the ambrosial nectar up
From lily, tulip, buttercup.

But 'tis not from the thornless rose
To us the sweetest odor flows ;
In the dark cloud the bow is set,
And love in tears is lovelier yet ;
Sorrow rejoices in its sight,
And saddest faces are made bright.

Two ships are sailing on the sea,
Two hearts are beating earnestly,
   To gain the western sphere;
Two days apart, he first to start,
'Tis Arthur's voice we hear.

" I've turned the cape of Norway round,
  Mount Blanc with snowy honors crowned,
  I've trod beneath my feet, and heard
  Volcanoes when their wrath was stirred.
  I've roamed on Como's woody shore,
  And sailed the five Lakes o'er and o'er;
  Seen antique villas in their pride, ·
  Nestled upon the mountain-side,
  And tall, grim castles looking down
  With sullen, medieval frown;
  I've whiled away the happy hours
  In Switzern valleys robed in flowers,
  Where beauty's queenly step had pressed,—
  And every charm was loveliest;
  Blue-bells in clusters decked those spots,
  And myriads of forget-me-nots,
  Sweet violets of celestial grace,
  And buttercups with sunny face;

While down the mountain's rugged side
Leaps forth the cascade's roaring tide.
I've seen the goats, all black and white,
In columns marching up the height;
And I have passed the Simplon way,
Met nature in sublime display,
Beneath the sun-lit mountain peak
Beheld the clouds their fury break,
And sportive there play hide and seek;
From clouds looked down on vales below,
Where the meandering rivers flow,—
Roadways white,
As paved with light,
And upward to the cloudless snow.

" On Rhigi's top I took my seat,
The rumbling thunders 'neath my feet.—
There I beheld the great sunrise ;
Below me lay the lingering night,
Above, the heavens were blue and bright,
And far up in the Alpine height
I sought and found the Edelweiss !

" I've trod the ancient streets of Rome,
 And breathed its musty air,—
Where God's own temple is defaced,
 And Peter's is made fair.

" And when the venerated Pope
 Set blessing on my head,
I tossed the bauble to a child,
 And took its smile, instead.

" I've stood beside the ancient Nile,
 Swelling in all its pride,
And seen the armored crocodile
 Among its rushes hide.

"And I have swam the Hellespont,
 In ancient history famed,
And won the laurels, fresh and fair,
 That proud Leander claimed.

'· Viewed, at the palace of Versailles,
 Napoleon's army grand,
Repeating all their battles o'er,
 With gleaming sword in hand.

"And noble galleries of art,
    Oh, Raphael inspired !
Many Madonnas I have seen,
    But thine the most admired !

" Hour after hour I've watched each grace
    Unfolding beauty rare,
And every moment I could trace
    Some lurking wonder there.

" I've wandered round the Parthenon,
    On Athens' classic hills,
And drank the snows of Lebanon
    Flowing in crystal rills.

" And where the lofty Pyramids
    Arose with stately pride,
In sacred dread I bowed my head,
    An infant by their side.

" And I've roamed o'er Ireland green,
    And by the Lakes Killarney,
At the old castle I have seen
    And kissed that stone, the ' Blarney.'

"I've walked o'er Scotia's Highland ground
    And heather many a mile,
  And I have sailed Loch Katreen round,
    And touched ' fair Ellen's Isle.'

" From all I part for one fond heart,
    And bid each scene adieu,
  While visions blest, upon the west,
    Are rising to my view.

" The glories that I might repeat
    With my historic pen,
  And stories which, for reasons sweet,
    I will rehearse again.

" The old town mill that Brainard sung,
    And I remember seeing,
  But more the day and more the hour
    That I from it was fleeing,

" The meeting-house that floated down [5]
    The Thames, in former days,
  The frogs that leaped through Windham town,[C]
    Worthy the poet's lays,

" Putnam, who fought the prowling wolf,
　　And almost fought a duel, (7)
But not with pistol or with sword,
　　Leaving his name a jewel,

" The night I spent on Jacob's Rocks,
　　Tossed upward by the billow,
And saw the stars go forth in flocks,
　　And made the stone my pillow,

" Oh ! richer charms did I behold,
　　In one who dreamed of me,
Than dwells in beds of drifted gold,
　　Or grottoes of the sea,

" The graces for her brow have wrought
　　Their choicest diadem ;
Her silence is a golden thought,
　　Her speech the rarest gem,
I'd hold a kingly crown at naught
　　To touch her garment's hem."

Arthur is tossed upon the deep,
With booming wrath the billows leap,

Unlock the winds a thousand keys,
A storm arose which shook the seas,
Cyclone and whirlwind meeting cloud,
And thunders breaking long and loud ;
The darkness every heart appals,
On every face a horror falls,
While close within his hand was found
A little roll, which he unbound,
Written for Mabel's heart a song,
When winds were high and waves were strong.
These lines he read by lightning's glare
The vessel lurching everywhere :

" Amid the wailings of the sea,
  Mine as the dying swan's shall be,
  Its last, its sweetest melody.
  The tempest rages, with the flash
  Of lightning falls the deafening crash ;
  No welcome star of hope in sight,
  Black is the mantle of the night,
  But in my heart is one who sings :
' Could I but spread seraphic wings,
  A heavenly watcher I would be,
  To keep perpetual guard o'er thee.'

I know that voice, and God will hear
The prayer that's offered in his ear;
And every storm that I outride
Shall bear me nearer to thy side."

No cloud is seen; the weary gales
Are pillowed in the fanning sails,
Or gently wafting'o'er the sea
The spicy wealth of Araby.

On quiet waters borne along,
From Mabel's lips breaks forth this song:
"I sail upon the tranquil wave;
There's not a cloud in sight;
The rising sun bathes his fair brow,
And sets in ocean bright.
And lighted in the distant blue,
The lamps of heaven are shining through
The curtains of the night.
Oh! may my life forever be
Serene and placid as the sea
And cheerful as the light!

" On Naples far-famed bay I've seen,
    Purpling the eastern skies,
  The first glad ray of waking day,
    And hailed the bright sunrise.

" And low descending in the west,
    Beheld the mighty sun
  Lie glowing on the water's breast,
    As earth and heaven were one.

" And I have sailed when skies were clear,
    That city of the seas,
  Where gaily sang the gondolier
    And rose the palaces.

" Upon the borders of the Rhone
    I've plucked the perfumed flowers,
  And watched its flow by morning's glow
    And at the twilight hours.

" But I do love my own blue Thames
    E'er fed by living fountains,
  And noble streams of Indian names
    Upspringing in the mountains,

"All gliding through the valleys sweet
    To that delightful river,
  By airy wing of zephyr touched
    I've seen its waters quiver,
  While jauntily upon its breast
  My little skiff would rock and rest.
  And I have seen its quiet depths
    Reflecting cloud and sky,
  And gazed along its winding course
    Far as could reach the eye,
  Where nestled 'mid the distant hills
    Its cradled waters lie.
  I ne'er beheld a lovelier scene
  Or skies more bright, or hills more green,
  Or blissful morning more serene,
  While islands in the distance rest
  As emeralds on the water's breast.
  The traveler with admiring eyes
  Exclaims, ' Can this be Paradise ? '

"There towers that lofty monument
    On Groton's tragic height,
  To mark the spot where martyrs fell
    Undaunted in the fight.

" There Ledyard sleeps and many a score
    Of heroes each renowned,
  Who midst the battle's wildest roar
    Were firm and foremost found.

" Amid the storm of fire they sang
    ' Columbia shall be free,'
  And every whizzing bullet rang,
    For honor, liberty.

" Allyns and Edgecombs left their plow
    To win immortal fame,
  And glory sets on many a brow
    I need not call by name.

" Let Hempstead's memory be bright
    Who wrote the battle's story,
  Wounded and bruised and down the steep
    Hurled in that wagon gory,

" And left for dead among the dead
    Till touched by gentle hand,
  He saw his wife and rose again
    To live long in the land. (8)

    4

" 'Twas there Decatur with his fleet
 Held hostile ships at bay,
 And guarded well the sacred place
 Where patriot ashes lay.

" And fresh upon that famous shore
 Shall live the name of one,
 Who gave the garment that she wore
 As wadding for the gun. (9)

" There Uncas darted his canoe,
 A friendly Indian power,
 And there the Pequot warrior drew
 His bow in evil hour,

" And fell beneath the white man s wrath,
 As falls a stately tower,
 Yet, from the reddened earth, looks up
 To heaven the dewbright flower.

" And there that quaint old city stands,
 New London, on the Thames,
 With Groton looking from the east,
 All bearing British names.

" There may be found that ancient well
    In its perpetual flow,
Where a whole family once fell
    By the assassin's blow,
But one, who in the cradle lay,
    And father, who was far away ;
And from that little one has sprung
    Thousands, who live to-day.
Nobly for ·conscience' sake he fought,
    And kept his foes at bay ;
And still the light upon that shore
    Is bright with freedom's ray. (10)

" John Rogers, let his name be known,
    And hallowed lips repeat,
Trampled the fiery serpent down
    Of priestcraft 'neath his feet.

" From pure religion, rightly named,
    He never turned his face,
But ever earnestly proclaimed
    Its messages of grace.

" When David went with sling and stone,
　　The giant foe must fall;
Those heroes, standing in the sun,
　　Held victory at call.

" The equal right of all to choose
　　And worship as they please,
Poured from their lips with morning dews.
　　And sweetened every breeze. (11)

" On Margarita's rock-bound coast
　　An ocean steamer lay,
Broken and burned upon a reef.
　　Who was it passed that way?
The Meteor, a whaling-ship,
　　Was there without delay;
Brightly, among the highest stars,
　　The captain's name shall shine,
Who saved from bleak and barren rock,
　　And from the billowy brine,
Five hundred shipwrecked souls, and more;
　　His brow with laurels twine!

"Full fifty days upon the sea
  He sailed, with living freight,
Sinking himself to poverty,
  He stands among the great,
Who never yet withheld his aid,
  And never yet with gold was paid. (12)

"The first to cross the Atlantic's wave
  By Fulton's proud invention;
All honor to those sailors brave,
  And of their deeds make mention. (13)

"Their name upon the roll of fame
  A lofty place shall hold,
More brilliant set in memory
  Than all the gifts of gold
Bestowed by titled hands upon
  The navigators bold.

"A ship on fire! a ship on fire!
  The sea-born Briton cried,
Seeking to render friendly aid,
  With canvas spreading wide.

Our Yankees looked at them, and laughed,
And sped away their little craft
Without a sail, without an oar,
Its like they had not seen before;
And ere he touched the royal wharf,
   With pennant proudly streaming,
'Take down your banner,' cried John Bull,
   A commodore you 're seeming;
'Take down the pennant, and put up
   A broader in its place.'
The captain answered, with an air
   Defiant in his face,
  'Get ready the hot water pipes,
   Be sure you aim them right;'
The Englishman took lively hint
   And vanished out of sight.

"To wondering nations forth they go,
   Their memory enshrine,
The world moves on, move as it may,
   America is mine.

"Within its Thames a harbor lies
   Smooth as a summer lake,

Where like white swans the vessels speed
    Their safe repose to take,
When the dark omens of the sky
    Their fearful signals make.

" Oft in the deep secure recess,
    Sheltered by islands near,
As darkness draws its curtains round
    By hundreds they appear,
A phantom city of the sea
    With lanterns burning clear!

" There on a rock I stayed one night,
    Wide severed from the land,
And there I thought of Jacob's dream
    And of the angel band ;
I too could into heaven see—
    There was an angel stood by me.

" But islands fair, and rivers rare,
    Italian sunsets golden,
I heed them not to one so fair
    By sweetest ties I'm holden,
Nor fadeless palms nor music's charms
Shall longer keep me from his arms."

He by Minerva's hand is crowned
　With every shining thought,
His heart is like a sea profound
　Whence richest gems are brought,
And from his lips flow sweetest sound
　That ear has ever caught.

Behold a cloud upon the sky
Like that which met the prophet's eye,
Appears, not larger than a hand
Or raven's wing, see it expand.
It spreads to an enormous size,
In all directions now it flies,
On angry seas 'tis lowering down.
The seas retort the black'ning frown;
Winds bellow from their hollow caves,
Ocean majestic lifts its waves,
Destruction's sword is keenly whet,
The elements for battle set.
Their awful front the heavens bowed,
And God himself spake from the cloud:
He bade the lightnings show their face;
Oh God! where is thy dwelling place?

The deep'ning thunders rend the sky,
All nature answers, " God is nigh ! "
The mad tornadoes rumbling rise,
Adown the mast the lightning flies,
The moaning tempest wilder shrieks,
The battling thunder louder breaks,
The sky is filled with blazing ire,
The vessel's hold is now on fire !
The crinkling lightning cleaves the air,
Its forked tongues are everywhere.
Sea opens its ten thousand graves,
Each for its trembling victim raves ;
Thy channels then, O deep, were seen,
A thin veil them and death between !
What can they do ?   Where can they go ?
The vessel heaving to and fro.

Crowding the cabin you might see
A weird and ghastly company ;
Among all those so frantic there
Was Mabel knelt in fervent prayer,
Not for herself on that dread day,
For whom, perhaps, we need not say.

The wailing blasts their wails repeat,
Mad voices howling through the air
As if a million wolves were there,
Or all wild beasts had left their lair,
In one dire climax, meet and meet!
Dark surging billows rising higher,
In depths of horror they're immersed,
A mountain sea puts out the fire,
The winds are stilled, the clouds dispersed,
But where the other ship may be
Is hid in deepest mystery.

'Tis midnight, but the doleful hours
Are gladdened by the heavenly powers;
The moon appears in queenly state,
Sweet mercy's priests around her wait,
Casting a gleam across the wave ;
Light flies on swiftest wing to save.
What in the distance can it be ?
A vessel pitching in the sea ?
The waters hold it for their prey.
Before there dawns another day
Will ship and lives be swept away !
But Mabel's prayer was heard that night;

A welcome sail appears in sight;
Thanksgivings rise as incense sweet;
All lives are saved: the lovers meet
And with entrancing raptures greet.

MABEL.

My love is like the morning sun,
　That cheers the world with light,
His beams so fair to look upon
　They overcome my sight.

ARTHUR.

And thou art like the risen moon,
　That changes night to day,
And from the sun will never turn
　Her countenance away.

The great world shall pour all its stores at our
　　feet,
The sun, moon, and stars shall combine,
　The rocks and the hills
　And the murmuring rills
Shall whisper, thou art mine,
　By title grand,
　We understand.

MABEL.

And ocean waves, and coral caves,
Rivers and mountains,
Zephyrs and fountains,
Shall echo, I am thine.

ARTHUR.

While stars shall o'er us shine.

MABEL.

And when the stars shall cease to shine
Immortal love shall us entwine!

The ship rejoicing breasts the wave,
   Glad moments laughing fly,
Joy's brightest tear, like morning clear,
   Glistened in every eye.

"Help!" one has fallen in the sea;
A cry is heard, "Who can it be?"
Then Arthur plunged, as quick as thought,
And Mabel in his arms he caught,
And to the deck he safely brought.

The stately ship ploughs thro' the sea,
And songs of joy rise cheerily,
For life that's spared, and on they go ;
The raging storm has ceased to blow,
The sun shines out, and all is gay
And merry as a morn in May.

The perils of the ocean 'o'er,
They're landed on their native shore,
Where first they saw the morning's glow,
And felt love's pulses bounding flow,
And Mabel upward turned her eyes,
And looked so wistful to the skies !

Where at the dawn the dew was brightest,
And on the lawn her step was lightest,
'Mid scenes as fair and friends as true
As when to home they bade adieu.

BOOK IV.

As earliest flowers in Eden sprang
Among the bowers where angels sang;
By God's own hand to man was given,
The choicest, noblest gift of heaven.
And the first miracle we see
In Cana, land of Galilee,
Where Jesus made his face to shine,
And beautified the rite divine,
By turning water into wine.

The sun shone forth in all his might,
The world with beauteous gems was bright,
Blue skies upon the hill tops lay,
As heaven had bowed itself that day,
That Mabel gave her hand away.

The years have rolled their circuits round,
And age is with its honors crowned;

And hallowed joys their hearts entwine
Our Hero and our Heroine.

Although the leaf of life be sere,
It brightens with autumnal cheer.
And children's children's voices please,
Like those brought up on Jacob's knees.

As pure their love as flakes of snow
Which erst on Salmon lay;
Fair, as the colors of the bow;
Serene as twilight's ray.

Behold a picture of their thought:
Past, present, future, all inwrought!

ARTHUR.

I deemed the bird that sweetly sung
Upon the cherry tree
Before the door, when I was young,
The happiest of the feathered throng;
Because it sung for me.

It watched the purpling gates of day,
It tuned aloft its matin lay

And poured its joyous minstrelsy
In notes so full and clear;
Though circling spheres,
Have measured years,
Its merry song I hear.

And well I loved the murmuring streams,
The stars that o'er me shone
So beautiful in childhood's dreams;
   And sylvan bowers,
   And breath of flowers,
And these were all my own!

MABEL.

I thought the rose at morn, so fair,
   In glory was complete;
But on the dewy evening air,
   Its perfume is more sweet.

And flowers which hide away at night;
   As touched with shade of sorrow,
Only conceal their beauties bright,
   To smile again to-morrow.

Hope, on the fadeless stars is set,
  That hail us from the sky,
And stars there are, which never yet
  Were seen by mortal eye.

ARTHUR.

The gleeful birds are singing still,
  And blossoms gem the lea ;
There's music in the flowing rill,
  And still it flows for me.

The earth is green beneath my tread
  And zephyrs fan my bower,
And stars are clear above my head,
  As in life's morning hour.

E'en in the cloud there is a light
  As we shall see at last,
When we ascend above the clouds,
  That life have overcast.

MABEL

From clouds which darken all the sky,
  The welcome rain is given,

And flowerets spring within the cleft,
   That by the bolt is riven.
The world, whichever way we look,
Is always touched by heaven!

ARTHUR.

And when thick vapors round us rise,
   So dense we dare not move,
We watch for God's resplendent skies
   To light us from above;
And in His sun we brighter see
   The tokens of His love.

MABEL.

Fair weather cometh from the north;
   In ice the crystals glow;
But for the mists which mantle earth
   There'd be no vestal snow,
And that dear flower, the Edelweiss,
   Its face would never show.
Instruction round our pathway gleams,
   Whichever way we go,

And goodness flows in countless streams,
   And mercies overflow;
And love, which reigns within our hearts,
   Makes brighter all below,
And tears of grief which fall at night,
At morn, are turned to dewdrops bright;
   Have we not found it so?

ARTHUR.

God over all extends his care,
And every germ sends up its prayer.

MABEL.

And every bud from censer meet,
Offers to heaven its incense sweet.

ARTHUR.

The forests wear a crown of praise,
Made golden in the autumn days.

MABEL.

And all around are emblems bright,
Of Heaven, dawning on our sight.

ARTHUR.

The Book of God is nature's book,
In which the wise delight to look.

MABEL.

And in the Bible, where we trace
The brighter glories of his grace.
Of pure religion let me hear
Something that shall delight my ear.

ARTHUR.

Doing the will of God is all
That pure religion we may call;
The moon looks ever to the sun;
Be true to God, your duty's done.

MABEL.

Yet sends the moon to earth the light
That shines upon her face so bright.

ARTHUR.

So shall our deeds in darkness shine,
Reflecting ever light divine.

MABEL.

And what distinction may we draw
Between Religion and the Law?

ARTHUR.

Religion and the law are one;
As colors flowing from the sun
In perfect harmony unite,
All blending in the purest white.

MABEL.

Far more to be desired than gold,
   Are all thy precepts, Lord;
And sweeter to our longing taste
   Than honey, is Thy word.

ARTHUR.

We must mark well the Saviour's steps,
While on the earth we go.

MABEL.

To those who seek to keep his ways
He will his footprints show.

ARTHUR.

And we shall mount on eagles' wings;
While waiting on the Lord.

MABEL.

"And we shall reign with Him as king,"
'Tis written in his word.

ARTHUR.

We're standing on the crystal sea,
   Before the throne we bow;
There is no future and no past,
   But one Eternal Now.
Death dies, not we, and in that hour
We yield to him, he yields his power;
Immortal life we here receive;
Passing Death's portals, still we live.

MABEL

And will the spirit take its flight
Through distant space, to worlds of light?

ARTHUR.

If God's our dwelling place below,
We surely have not far to go;

'Tis in the soul that heaven lies,
And not far off beyond the skies.

MABEL

Speak to me of the world to come,
That is so soon to be our home.

ARTHUR

We shall be with him where he is,
Behold his face, partake his bliss,
Beneath life's tree, by life's pure river,
Out of the throne proceeding ever.

MABEL

E'en here we walk the streets of gold,
And God in all his works behold.
And Death itself shall have no sting,
And victory o'er the grave we sing.
Shall we in that blest sphere above
Meet and converse with those we love?

ARTHUR.

'Twas Moses and Elias talked
    With Jesus, face to face,
And angels speed their way to earth,
    With messages of grace.

And is not God forever near,
Doth not his love our souls insphere ?—
Nor breadth nor thickness, hath the line
That separates from things divine.

The new Jerusalem comes down ;
  We drink its consolations,
Its stones are laid with colors fair,
  Pure sapphires its foundations.
Into its open gates is brought
  The glory of the Nations.

MABEL.

To see thy brightness, kings shall come,
  And at thy feet shall bow ;
O Zion, city beautiful !
  Joy of the world art thou :
The box, the fir-tree, and the pine
  Shall beautify thy brow.

ARTHUR

And I was glad they said to me
  Come thou, and let us go
Up to the House of God ; for there
  His beauty he will show.

5

MABEL

Ofttimes I've felt a boding fear
That my last hours might not be clear.

ARTHUR.

As pillowed on the western sky,
I saw the moon serenely lie,
A darksome cloud was hovering near.
It rose and left the heavens all clear,
And soon that cloud became so bright
And roseate with the tints of light,
Dissolving it was lost to sight.
'Twas then I heard my spirit say,
Thus fear's dark cloud shall melt away,
Tinged with the glow of parting day.

MABEL.

Bright faces we have seen before
Shall greet us at the pearly door,
And little feet may be will guide
Us closer to the Saviour's side.

ARTHUR

The golden sunsets through the trees!
Sweet nature lends such charms as these

To show that earth is interlaced
With heaven, or is by heaven embraced.

MABEL.

What of the resurrection morn?

ARTHUR.

The glorious day of night is born,
Life springs from Death it is decreed,
Behold the germinating seed!
Hid in the chrysalis doth lie
The splendors of the butterfly.
And in God's word 'tis plainly read,
That Christ is risen from the dead;
So in his likeness we shall rise,
Caught up to meet Him in the skies.

MABEL

And all the beauties we behold,
  In things which greet our eyes,
Are types of glory to unfold
  Where beauty never dies.

ARTHUR.

Of all which thou hast given me,
   We hear the Saviour say,
I have lost nothing, but will raise
   It up at the last day.

MABEL.

And evermore the immortal soul,
Its jewel shall enshrine,
And all the sweet affinities
That here our hearts entwine.
There prattling tongues to us will tell
The glories of Emanuel!
What then, will our employment be.
We may not lift the veil to see.

ARTHUR.

To serve our God with all our might,
And find in Him our chief delight,
'Tis heaven upon the earth below,
And will be heaven when hence we go.
Pursuits, as various as our thought,
Will doubtless to our hand be brought,
And faith which bears us on its wings,

From which all holy virtue springs ;
The hope that in our bosom sings,
And love, with its divinest glow,
Shall mingle in that emerald bow,
Which evermore surrounds the throne
Of worship, praise to God alone.
Our earthly light but fades away,
To merge in bright unending day.

MABEL.

So 1 have seen the moon retire
Upon her couch of blue,
'Mid glories of the rising morn
Not lost, but hid from view.

ARTHUR.

There's nothing lost in nature's vast domain,
Flowers bloom to die, and die to bloom again,
And shall a loss within the soul be found,
While none there is creation's realm around ;
The goings forth of morn are still as bright
As when they gladdened Eden's primal night.

MABEL

And love's own star, the seal of heaven,
Is set upon the brow of Even.

ARTHUR

I'm seventy-one years old to-day.

MABEL

And I am sixty-seven,
And still my heart is young and gay
As when I was eleven,
And nature wears as charming grace
As when the ship came through the Race!

ARTHUR

The rising beauties of the morn
With rosy fingers paint the dawn.

MABEL

Yet richer glories hath the west
As Earth's great bridegroom seeks his rest.
And nature weaves, with golden thread,
The curtains of his royal bed.

ARTHUR.

Age adds but splendor to the soul
Where love majestic holds control.
 The winter rose is rarest ;
 The autumn leaf is fairest.
Behold the forest's blazoned glow.
Descending sun reveals the bow.

MABEL.

And violets open their bright eyes
To look on January skies.
Although the snows their petals press,
They part with naught of loveliness.

ARTHUR.

On the celestial hills above,
 There spring immortal flowers,
Transplanted from that land of love,
 They gladden earthly bowers.
But one there is that stands confessed,
The fairest, sweetest, loveliest.
Live on, bright flower, as thou wert given,
First in the smiling wreath of heaven !

MABEL.

Forever blooming near the skies,
The Flower of Love, my Edelweiss!

ARTHUR

Love makes this world a paradise!

MABEL.

Why don't the mighty gospel shine,
　　As shines the glorious sun,
Through the dark corners of the earth,
　　Enlightening every one?
Why the grim ages on us spring,
Just as we hear the angels sing?

ARTHUR

When you explain the mystery
　　That's hidden in the dew,
And tell me how it holds its form,
　　Seeing its nature through,
And all the laws that govern it,
　　Then I will answer you.
Of God's great plan, the part is small
That's known upon this earthly ball;
Not many things transparent be,
'Tis but the surface that we see.

MABEL.

If things on Earth are pre-ordained,
How can our freedom be maintained?

ARTHUR.

Perhaps the freedom that we call
Lies as the corner-stone of all.

MABEL.

If man were free, why do we pray
That he should be restrained? Please say.

ARTHUR.

As leaping down the mountain's side,
I saw a sportful streamlet glide,
Sped on by an inherent force,
It sang of freedom in its course.
" I steer my way to yonder sea,
Part of the ocean I shall be."—
But, lightly touched by human hand,
It spread, and watered all the land.
Did not that streamlet flow as free
As when it sought the distant sea?
In heaven and earth are things supreme,
Of which "Horatio" did not dream.

MABEL.

What of the change within us wrought,
That we are in the Scriptures taught?

ARTHUR.

From glory unto glory we
Are changed, as Jesus' face we see.

MABEL.

What's orthodoxy to your mind?

ARTHUR.

Faith, hope, and charity combined,
With every royal virtue twined.—
Knowledge is ignorance refined,
Seeming to know both this and that,
It flits in darkness like a bat,
Not rightly named, 'tis folly's speech
The knowledge that I here impeach.
Of the trackless, boundless sea,
God's infinite immensity,
What do we know?   What can we tell?
'Tis high as heaven, 'tis deep as hell.

MABEL.

The knowledge that's from heaven descended
Is with all moral beauty blended.

ARTHUR.

Upon the Word we safely rest,
As John, upon the Saviour's breast.
Our Father's hand to us is given,
The little child is type of heaven!

MABEL.

Why in the Bible should there be
Things seeming contradictory?

ARTHUR.

In nature it is just the same;
Truth is a parti-colored flame!
Water, we say, will run down hill,
Water, in vapor, rises still.
Reflected in the drop of dew
One sees the red, and one the blue.

MABEL

How can we turn our eyes away
From yonder sun, and calmly say,
Farewell, thou glorious orb of day?

ARTHUR

Our God is all, and He will see
The sun for us, where'er we be;
All things are ours, in loftiest sense;
Omniscience, and omnipotence.

MABEL.

And we do all things here possess
In Christ, the " Lord, our Righteousness."

ARTHUR

Great are Thy works, Almighty King!
  And wondrous to behold;
Summer and Winter, Autumn, Spring,
  Thy majesty unfold!

Day unto day shall utter speech;
  Night unto night make known;
And every grain of sand to preach
  Has orders from Thy throne.

Thy witnesses are gone abroad,
  Each leaf its story tells;
And holiness unto the Lord,
  Is written on the bells.

MABEL.

And though to scale the hills of thought,
  Mortals in vain essay,
The highest lessons we are taught,
  To worship and obey.

TOGETHER.

Father in heaven, look down,
  And take away each stain,
Place on our head the crown,
  With thee on earth to reign.

And when thou call'st us hence,
  May we rejoicing go,
    And take our seat
    Near to the feet
  Of Him we loved below.

The glorious word to earth was sped
  When first it saw the sun,
A man unto his wife shall cleave
  And they twain shall be one!
In the beginning it was said,
  Let the commandment run

Through all the ages of the world,
    Till time itself is done :—
But love shall last when time is o'er,
    And brighter bloom forevermore!

Through all life's journey, hand in hand,
Thus Arthur and his Mabel stand ;
An Eden sweet is here their home,
Their earnest of the one to come.
In service, prayer and praise, they see
Of glory, the celestial key ;
Though trials line their pathway here,
And every dew-drop be a tear ;
They never of their sorrows tell·—
In Baca's valley springs a well.

See they not God in all their ways,
Are they not living to his praise ?
And on his will do they not wait
As watchers at the morning's gate ?
The law of truth within their heart
Shall never from their mouth depart,
And children shall to theirs repeat
The counsels of their lips most sweet.

Of mercy and of truth they sing,
To God their humble offerings bring,
At morning, noon, and evening hour,
As breathes the fragrance of the flower,
Their hands are swift and warm their heart
The grateful succour to impart.
For beauty in the words they see,
" What touches man, relates to me."

Songs from the utmost parts shall swell,
    Circling the earth around ;
Who drinks from truth's eternal well,
    With glory shall be crowned.

In the Almighty they delight,
    They on high places ride ;
Horses and chariots of light
    Are waiting by their side.

As blushful is retiring day,
    As sweet the scented bower,
As gladsome morning's earliest ray,
    As still the midnight hour ;

As when they met among the hills,
  And Mabel wore that flower!

As fresh, the incense roses throw,
  As pure the crystal dew;
And living fountains for them flow,
  To cheer their journey through.
For neither time nor age we know
  Where God makes all things new.

The pillar of the fire by night,
  And of the cloud by day
Is ever set before their sight
  To lead them on their way.
As nearer unto God they draw,
  They love him more and more;
They see no temple and no sun,
  But Him, whom they adore.

Their sun shall never more go down,
  Nor moon its brightness hide;
They in God's everlasting light
  And glory shall abide!

The Twain whose hearts were linked in love,
  On earth no more are seen;
By life's clear river now they rove
  On banks of living green.

From that high sphere, still sounding near,
  Their song is ever sweet;—
But echoes of the heavenly land
  We may not here repeat.

FINIS.

NOTES.

NOTE 1.—page 9.

While half the commerce of the world
Is passing at thy feet.

More vessels pass over Long Island Sound than over any like expanse of water on the globe, the British Channel perhaps excepted.

NOTE 2.—page 28

Where lofty mountains touch the skies,
I plucked for thee this Edelweiss.

"There is a flower known to botanists, one of the same genus with our summer plant called 'Life Everlasting,' a *gnaphalium* like that, which grows on the most inaccessible cliffs of the Tyrolese mountains, where the chamois dare hardly venture, and which the hunter, tempted by its beauty and by his love (tor it is immensely valued by the Swiss maidens), climbs the cliffs to gather, and is sometimes found dead at the foot with the flower in his hand.   It is called by botanists the *Gnaphalium contopodium*, but by the Swiss, EDELWEISSE, which signifies *Noble Purity* "—*Ralph Waldo Emerson.*

"The Edelweiss is an alpine plant that is said to grow on the line of perpetual snow,—in fact under the snow.   Only the boldest alpine goatherds and hunters venture to pick the hardy little plant from its native soil.   The possession of one is a proof of unusual daring   It is a peculiar plant of delicate construction, and containing very little sap, so that it can be preserved a long while, like our everlasting.   The blossom is surrounded by white velvety leaves, and even the stem has a down upon it. The Latin name is *Leontopodium alpinum*, which means alpine lion's-foot."—*Berthold Auerbach.*

THE EDELWEISS

I was born in my little shroud,
　All woolly, warm, and white,
I live in the mist and cloud,
　I live for my own delight.

I see far beneath me crowd
　The alpine roses red,
That make the valleys bright,
　And the gentian blue, sun-fed.

I bloom for the eagle's eye,
　I bloom for the daring hand,
I live but for God, and I die
　Unto Him, and at His command.

　　　　　　　　　—Anon.

NOTE 3.—page 38.

By ancient mill tall trees around, etc.

This ancient mill is romantically located in the northern part of the city of New London, among rocks, embowering trees, and flowing waters, a picturesque scene at all seasons of the year. The story, though somewhat decorated, has a truthful basis.

NOTE 4.—page 53.

An isle of rocks is near us.

Jacob's rocks, so called, a small island of rocks in the Thames about a mile from New London

NOTE 5.—page 67.

The meeting-house, that floated down
The Thames, in former days.

The Bridgeport paper of March, 1823, said: "Arrived, the schooner Fame, from Charleston via New London. While at anchor in that harbor, during the rain storm on Thursday evening last, the Fame was run afoul of by the wreck of the Methodist meeting-house from Norwich, which was carried away in the late freshet." This fact called forth the following fragment from the New London poet Brainard, at the time of its occurrence:

THE CAPTAIN.

Solemn he paced upon the schooner's deck,
And muttered of his hardships:—"I have been
Where the wild will of Mississippi's tide
Has dashed me on the sawyer;—I have sailed
In the thick night, along the wave-washed edge
Of ice, in acres, by the pitiless coast
Of Labrador; and I have scrap'd my keel
O'er coral rocks in Madagascar seas—
And often in my cold and midnight watch,
Have heard the warning voice of the lee shore
Speaking in breakers! Ay, and I have seen
The whale and sword-fish fight beneath my bow,
And when they made the deep boil like a pot,
Have swung into its vortex; and I know
To cord my vessel with a sailor's skill,
And brave such dangers with a sailor's heart
—But never yet upon the stormy wave,
Or where the river mixes with the main,
Or in the chafing anchorage of the bay,
In all my rough experience of harm,
Met I—a Methodist meeting-house!"

NOTE 6.—page 67.

Thy frogs that leaped through Windham Town.

"On a dark, cloudy, dismal night in the month of July, A. D. 1758, the inhabitants of Windham, a small town in the eastern part of Connecticut, had retired to rest, and for several hours all were wrapped in profound repose—when suddenly, soon after midnight, the slumbers of the peaceful inhabitants were disturbed by a most terrific noise in the sky right over their heads. At intervals, many supposed they could distinguish the calling out of the particular names, as of Cols. Dyer and Elderkin, two eminent lawyers, and this increased the general terror. The tumult still increasing, old and young poured forth into the streets, forgetful in their hurry and consternation of their habiliments!"—*Hist. Coll. Conn.*

This tale of the Windham frogs, whatever were the facts upon which it is based, has been sung by humorists and perpetuated in picture on the bank bills of that town. Having so many ludicrous features in itself, exaggeration in telling the story seems to have been considered a merit From an unpublished ballad on the subject the following extract is taken:

> A negro man, a faithful man,
>   His name I have forgot,
> Was first to wake, and first to hear,
>   And heard he knew not what.
>
> "Arise! Arise!" aloud he cries,
>   "I'm sure there's something coming,
> About my head, upon my bed
>   I heard an awful drumming."
>
> "Awake! Awake! for your own sake,'
>   Then rushed he to the street,
> A better crier in time of fire
>   You'd very rarely meet.

The people rose and seized their clothes,
　As many as could find them,
And not a few if rumor's true,
　Their garments left behind them.

Not knowing why or where to fly
　The soldier seized his rifle,
The sexton well did ring the bell,
　The uproar was no trifle.

Col. Dyer! Col. Dyer! in every one's ear,
　Sounded louder and higher,
With a voice round and clear,
　Col. Dyer! Col. Dyer!

Elderkin, too! Elderkin, too!
　Rang out on every side,
" At last these crafty lawyers
　Are going to be tried!"

For so indeed the people thought,
　And so thought they.　Alack!
And made good resolution
　To pay the money back.

Confusion rare rose on the air,
　The scene it was appalling,
And some declared the sky itself
　Upon their heads was falling.

The parson he began to preach
　To the affrighted band,
But soon gave out, for want no doubt,
　Of words at his command.

And 'tis averred, as I have heard,
    That penitential tears!
Did fall apace, from many a face
    That had been dry for years.

If Dyer and Elderkin are called,
    Whose turn will it be next?
Some moaning said, and looked around
    As mortals much perplexed.

The welkin rang, some prayed, some sang
    As meet to the occasion;
And some there were who cried, "Prepare
    For barbarous invasion!"

The drum was beat, the roll was called,
    The cannon all were mounted;
And every one that had a gun
    Was there to have it counted.

"Soldiers in arms!" the captain cries,
    "Brave soldiers, all attend:
This very night you are to fight,
    Your honor to defend!

"We hear the tramp—the horrid yell
    Is sounding on the air.
They come! they come! with roll of drum,
    Like men for war prepare!

"Make ready all, take aim, and fire!
    They'll scatter at the sound."
The enemy returns salute:
    "You'd better go around!"

Again, again the voice is heard—
  "You 'd better go around."
"Stand still! stand still!" the captain cries,
  "Be firm—maintain your ground!

"And have you never heard the tale
  About Thermopylæ—
How the bold Spartan fought and fell,
  That Greece might still be free?

"And how, with his three hundred men,
  The brave Leonidas
Xerxes and all his hosts defied,
  Guarding that sacred pass!"

At every word each heart is stirred—
  Their courage rising higher;
Till, long before the speech was o'er,
  They all began to fire!

"Think how the great Miltiades"—
  His voice the captain raises;
And for their hasty firing
  Their ardent valor praises.

"Think how the great Miltiades,
  On far-famed Marathon,
Dashed down the Persian in his pride,
  And deathless glory won!"

Through brier and bush—on, on, they push—
  Such valorous deeds were wrought!
While hosts of frogs leaped from the bogs—
  No other foe they fought.

6

There was a pond, a noble pond,
　　Not distant from the place,
Which frogs had long inhabited—
　　An ancient, croaking race.

And still the oldest citizen
　　Had never known before
The day or date that it had failed
　　In years at least threescore.

That summer's sun had parched the earth,
　　The springs and streams were dry ;
Those frogs must leave their native home—
　　They must have drink, or die !

In marshaled band they crossed the land,
　　Their voices loud and grum ;
Which sounded not unlike, it seems,
　　The beating of a drum.

So well and lustily they call
　　Each honored lawyer's name,
That, by these frogs, they are inscribed
　　Upon the roll of fame.

With choral song they leap along,
　　They plunge into the river;
Which, more than all the pomp of war,
　　Did Windham town deliver.

NOTE 7.—page 68.

Putnam, who fought the prowling wolf,
　　And almost fought a duel—

General Putnam's military exploits are well known, as, also,

his descent into the wolf's den. From an original ballad,
recounting some incidents of his life, the following is quoted:

> Our hero once accepted
>   A challenge to a duel;
> Provided he might choose the arms—
>   Or, rather, choose the fuel.
>
> A braggart English officer
>   Had claimed to take offence;
> And to hide his want of courage
>   He showed his want of sense.
>
> But Putnam, at the appointed hour,
>   Sat down beside a barrel—
> Which seemed with powder to be filled—
>   Thus to avenge the quarrel!
>
> " Sit on the other side," said he,
>   "Your chance's as good as mine"—
> Lighting a match—the officer
>   Of fear displayed some sign.
>
> And just before the fire had crept
>   To where the powder lay,
> The valiant sprig of chivalry
>   Jumped up and ran away.
>
> "Ah! Ah!" quoth Putnam; "now I know
>   You are a coward, well;
> You bravely talk of powder,
>   Yet you do not like the smell!

> " The barrel, that you so much feared,
>   Is but with onions filled ,
> And on the top, to try you by,
>   A little powder spilled ! "

NOTE 8 —page 73

Let Hempstead's memory be bright
Who wrote the battle's story, etc.

Mr. Stephen Hempstead, the person here alluded to, was severely wounded at the storming of Fort Griswold, Sept. 6, 1781. The following is an extract from the narrative which he gave of that awful scene:

"After the massacre, they plundered us of everything we had. When they commenced gathering us up, together with their own wounded, they put theirs under the shade of the platform, and exposed us to the sun, in front of the barracks, where we remained over an hour. Those that could stand were then paraded and ordered to the landing, while those that could not—of which I was one—were put into one of our ammunition wagons and taken to the brow of the hill, which was very steep and at least one hundred rods in descent; from whence it was permitted to run down by itself, but was arrested in its course, near the river, by an apple tree. The pain and anguish we all endured by this rapid descent, as the wagon jumped and jostled over rocks and holes, is inconceivable, and the jar in the arrest was like bursting the cords of life asunder."

He was found by his wife and taken to the house of a brother—his own being laid in ashes—and after a year or so recovered. In 1811, he removed to St. Louis, where his son Edward had preceded him, and who became eminent as a lawyer there, and was the first delegate from Missouri Territory to

Congress. A younger son settled in Galena, Ills., and was senior law partner with Hon. Elihu B. Washburne, United States senator from Illinois, late minister to France, and whose wife is a grand-daughter of Stephen Hempstead. In an address delivered by Mr. Washburne, 1881, on the occasion of the presentation of the portrait of Hon. Edward Hempstead to the State of Missouri, he said of the father, Stephen Hempstead. " He was a man of much intelligence, of the strictest probity, and was possessed of all the elements of the best type of New England character. He was universally respected, and died lamented by all who had known him "

NOTE 9.—page 74.

Who gave the garment that she wore
As wadding for the gun, etc.

The name of Mrs. Bailey, of Groton, Conn., has become historic in consequence of the patriotic act here referred to.

NOTE 10 —page 75.

There may be found that ancient well
In its perpetual flow, etc.

The well referred to is situated a few rods north of the present limits of the city of New London, on the Norwich road, near the house of the late Captain Lyman Allyn. Thomas Bolles, son of Joseph Bolles, of Wells, Maine, a deputy and commissioner of that colony, at the invitation of Governor Winthrop, removed to New London, and in 1668 settled on the tract of land known to this day as Bolles' Hill; his residence being adjacent to the above named well On the evening of June 6, 1678, his wife and two children were murdered by a

vicious boy of sixteen, during Mr. Bolles' absence from home.
John Bolles, an infant of nine months, was spared and found
rolling in his mother's blood.   He in after life became famous
as an advocate of Christian liberty, and wrote a book entitled
" Liberty of Conscience In Bondage To No Flesh." Another of
his books is called " Good News From A Far Country," which
was written to prove that civil governments "have no au-
thority from God to Judge in Cases of Conscience." He wrote
also "A Brief Account of Persecutions in Boston and Connecti-
cut Governments," when eighty years of age. From 1708 to
1754, hardly a year elapsed without his assailing the abuses of
the established church, and vindicating the great principle of
" soul-liberty."

His study of the New Testament convinced him that slavery
is unchristian, and he manumitted all his slaves ; providing
generously for their support, and watching, all his life long,
over their welfare. His biographer states that " at the age of
thirty he became dissatisfied with the tenets of the Church in
which he had been educated.   That church was the only one
recognized by law. Its members composed the 'standing or-
der,' and from the foundation of the Colony until the adoption
of a State Constitution and the principle of religious liberty
in 1818, every person in Connecticut, whatever his creed, was
compelled to belong to, or pay taxes for the support of 'the
standing order.' It was as complete an 'Establishment' as
is the 'Established Church of England.'   Well educated,
familiar with the Bible, independent in fortune, earnest in his
convictions, and of a proselyting spirit, bold and fond of dis-
cussion, Mr. Bolles engaged very actively in polemical contro-
versy, and wrote and published many books and pamphlets."
"Once a year, as a general rule, he mounted his horse, with
saddle-bags stuffed full of books, and rode from county to

county, challenging discussion. He even made a pilgrimage to Boston, Mass., in 1754, to move the General Court of Massachusetts in this behalf, as he had often endeavored to move the Connecticut Legislature. This last exploit—a horseback ride of 200 miles in his 77th year—may be regarded as a fit climax to a long life of zealous effort in the cause of truth."

His biographer also says : "From one of his books it appears that his escape when his mother and her two other children were murdered, and his deliverance from other imminent perils, ' when,' to use his own words, ' there was but a hair's breadth between me and death,' made a deep impression on his mind, and made him feel that God had spared him for some special work. This belief he expressed in some homely verses, Bunyan-like in sound :

'I formerly did lose a tender mother ;
I also had a sister and a brother ,
My mother she was murdered with the rest,
And I, a babe, found sucking at her breast.
Yet was my life preserved by God's almighty hand,
Who since has called me forth for his great truth to stand.'

"Under the spur of this conviction he devoted himself to the great cause of religious freedom, encountering opposition and persecution, and suffering fines, imprisonments, and beating with many stripes. There is a record of proceedings in July, 1725, before a magistrate of Norwich, Conn., against John Bolles, his son Joseph, and others, charged with Sabbath-breaking; by which it appears that for going on Sunday from Groton and New London to attend Baptist worship in Lebanon, they were arrested on Sunday, imprisoned till the next day and then heavily fined ; the sentence being, that if fine and costs were not paid, they should be flogged on the bare back for non-payment of fine, and then lie in jail till payment of costs. As none of them would pay, they were all flogged —women as well as men—John Bolles receiving fifteen stripes, each of the others ten. Deputy Governor Jenks of Rhode Island, where the seeds of religious liberty had been sown by Roger Williams, having obtained a copy of these proceedings, ordered it to be publicly posted in Providence, and appended to it an indignant official proclamation."

The descendants of John Bolles have been among the foremost advocates of religious freedom in this State. The famous Baptist petition asking for equality of rights in matters pertaining to religion, was written by Judge David Bolles of Ashford, a copy of which in his own handwriting is extant. The narrator of his life says: "He was a Methodist in religion, and to his long continued and zealous services as advocate of the Baptist petition before successive legislatures, is Connecticut largely indebted for the establishment of religious liberty and the incorporation of the principle of uniform toleration into the State Constitution. An anecdote, illustrative of this point, may here be told. When these reformatory measures were being earnestly discussed, the late Calvin Goddard, then a young lawyer, said to David Bolles, Judge of the Court, at the dinner-table, 'You will blow your Baptist ram's horn till the walls of Jericho fall!' And he told the truth. The principles, once so unpopular, and strongly advocated by men in advance of their times, in the face of great opposition, have since become a fundamental part of the law of the land, and the brightest feature of modern Christian civilization."

It is but just to say that the Presbyterian or Congregational church, which constituted the tyrannical "standing order" of former times, is now among the foremost defenders of civil and Christian liberty.

NOTE 11.—page 76.

John Rogers, the bold assailant of ecclesiastical assumption, was born in 1648, and continued in the "standing order" until he was 25 years of age, when he adopted Baptist sentiments and became a Baptist teacher. A fine of £5 was then imposed upon every one who should administer the rite of baptism by immersion, and a fine of 20s. for non-attendance on the worship of the dominant church. For non-conformity to the rules of the church, he suffered fines, imprisonment, and whipping, with others of like faith. The persecution of dissenters was not carried as far in the New London plantation as at Boston, where fidelity to their religious convictions on the part of the Quakers, was punished with death. John Rogers at New London was foremost in resisting the unrighteous encroachments upon liberty of conscience, and suffered perhaps more than any other one on that account. It is not to be denied that if our Puritan ancestors had great virtues, they had also great faults; failing to realize the idea of Lord Bacon, when he said: "Character should be like a flower—all its parts evenly and beautifully enfolded together."

NOTE 12.—page 77.

Brightly among the brightest stars
The captain's name shall shine, etc.

Captain Samuel Jeffrey of the whale-ship Meteor from New London, at great sacrifice to himself and loss of his voyage, rescued the persons referred to

NOTE 13.—page 77.

The first to cross th' Atlantic wave,
By Fulton's proud invention, etc.

The Savannah, the first steamship that crossed the Atlantic

ocean, sailed from Savannah, Ga., on the 26th May, 1819, for Liverpool. Capt. Moses Rogers, a person of great mechanical skill and ingenuity, who had been familiar and identified with the experiments of Fulton, and Capt. Stevens Rogers, a thorough and practical sailor, both of New London, Conn., were its chief officers. The passage to Liverpool was made in 22 days.

"During the voyage across the Atlantic several amusing incidents occurred, but we have room only for the two following, obtained directly from the officers in command: When the ship was approaching Cape Clear, under steam, she was discovered by the officers of the telegraph station, and was reported to the admiral in command at Cork as a ship on fire. The admiral at once dispatched a fast cutter, well manned, to her relief; but great was their wonder at their total inability, under all sail and with a good breeze, to come up with a ship under "bare poles." After several shots had been fired from the cutter, the engine of the ship was stopped and the cutter permitted to approach, when her officers were invited on board to examine and admire the new invention. Soon after dropping her anchor in the harbor of Liverpool, a boat, manned with sailors in naval uniform, commanded by a lieutenant, came alongside, and the officer in a tone more authoritative than pleasing, demanded of the first man he saw, 'Where is your master?' 'I have no master,' replied the American. 'Where is your captain, then, sir?' 'He is below, sir,' was the reply. On reaching the deck Capt. Rogers asked the Englishman what he wanted. The officer replied, 'My commander demands to know by what authority you wear that pennant, sir?' pointing with his sword to a coach-whip pennant flying at the mainmast head. To this the captain replied, 'By the authority of my government, which is republican and permits me to do so.'

The officer then remarked that his commander considered it an insult to him, and commanded the American to haul down the pennant, intimating that if it was not quickly done he would be supplied with help. This was a little too harsh for Yankee spirit to endure, and Rogers instantly gave the order to 'haul down the coach-whip, and to supply its place with a broad blue pennant,' such as were worn by the commanders of squadrons in our own navy, and ranking with the highest grade in that of the British, and then in a loud tone of voice—so that he might be heard by the English—he directed the engineer 'to get the hot water pipes ready.' 'This order had the desired effect, although there was no such apparatus on board, and the 'gallant' lieutenant and his crew pulled for dear life. The hot water 'jeers' which were subsequently leveled at the British officers, caused them to start upon an early cruise.

"The Savannah attracted great attention at Liverpool; was visited by the authorities, and, as her fame spread to London, the crown officers, noblemen, and many leading merchants visited her. The officers were very anxious to ascertain her speed, her errand, and her destination. It was suspected by some that her design was to rescue Napoleon Bonaparte, then a prisoner at St. Helena, his brother Jerome having offered for that purpose a large sum. She was carefully watched by the British government, and ships of war were stationed at certain points for that purpose, which for a time prevented her departure from Liverpool.

"She finally proceeded to Copenhagen, where she excited great manifestations of wonder and curiosity. Thence she proceeded to Stockholm, where she was visited by the royal family, ministers of state, and naval officers, who by invitation, dined on board, and took an excursion among the neighboring islands, with which they were delighted. She then proceeded to St. Petersburg, having on board as a passenger one Lord Lyndock, who was so much pleased with the performance of the steamship that he presented to each of her officers some token of his esteem. To her sailing master was presented an elegant snuff box of pure and massive gold, on the cover of which, inlaid in platina, was a representation of Peter the Great asleep upon his horse, standing on the rock from which he viewed the Swedish army, with the serpent biting the heel of the horse, which awoke him in time to successfully attack the Swedes. At the bottom of the snuff box was this inscription: 'Presented by Sir Thomas Graham, Lord Lyndock, to Stevens Rogers, sailing master of the steamship Savannah, at St. Petersburg, October 10, 1819.' Lord Lyndock had taken passage on the steamer by invitation of Christopher Hughes, then American minister to Sweden. Upon her arrival at St. Petersburg, the vessel was visited by the entire court, who tested her qualities by a trip to Cronstadt, and so well pleased was the emperor, that he caused the officers to be treated with marked attention. They were invited to be present at a review of eighty thousand troops by the emperor in person; and a frigate of the largest class was launched on the 'camels' and taken down to Cronstadt as an exhibition of the progress of the arts in Russia. The emperor solicited Captain Stevens Rogers to remain in the Russian seas with his steamer, offering him the protection of the government and the exclusive navigation of the Black and Baltic Seas for a number of years; and to Captain Moses Rogers the emperor presented a handsome silver tea kettle. From St. Petersburg the Savannah sailed for Arendel, in Norway, and thence to Savannah, making the passage in 25 days. Thus ended the first voyage ever made across the Atlantic by a steamship."—*Round Table.*

CPSIA information can be obtained at www.ICGtesting.com
Printed in the USA
BVOW08s1217040814

361596BV00034B/1085/P